Purpose Is Calling

YOU

Passionately Pursuing Purpose

BY

VALERIE M TASI

PURPOSE IS CALLING YOU By Valerie M Tasi

Published by MO PUBLISHING

Mo.publishing@yahoo.com

First Edition 2021

PURPOSE IS CALLING YOU

ISBN- 978-1-64660-023-6

All scripture quotations, unless otherwise indicated, are taken from the New International Version.

Foreword

I have had the incredible opportunity to know Valerie for many years and watch her soar through life and all that it presents. She is creative, thoughtful, inspiring, and motivational in her approach to ministry and the things of God. She has the ability to capture you unaware many times due to her keen sensitivity and discernment in the spirit. She unapologetically lives life with a freedom in God that comes from intimately knowing Him and experiencing His glory. She has a tender and ready spirit for the things of God. Valerie is an intimate friend, and a humble submitted daughter full of passion & purpose whom I am dearly proud of. You will find her to be a true gift.

As you read, consider, and embrace these things presented in the book, you will find yourself being activated in your call to prayer and ministry. She will provoke intercession and passion for prayer and intimacy with the Father.

Bishop Ilinda Jackson

Secret Place Community Church

Oklahoma City, OK

Contents

Foreword --- iii

Dedication --- v

Acknowledgments -- vii

Introduction --- ix

Chapter 1: Beautifully Rooted In Christ ------------------------------- 1

Chapter 2: Purpose -- 6

Chapter 3: Who Am I --- 15

Chapter 4: Identity Crisis -- 25

Chapter 5: The Strength of a Woman ------------------------------- 33

Chapter 6: God is my Rock -- 40

Chapter 7: Preparation for his kingdom -------------------------- 48

Chapter 8: Worthy is the call -- 56

Chapter 9: Victorious Women --- 64

Chapter 10: From Tragedy to Triumph ----------------------------- 70

Chapter 11: When Purpose Pursues YOU -------------------------- 79

Chapter 12: I am a Gift -- 86

Dedication

I would like to dedicate this book to my niece Promise, known as my Princess. I have seen you be so resilient in life; you have had one tough journey, I have watched you have seasons where you have bloomed and blossomed, and I have seen you go through some of your darkest hours. But you keep fighting the good fight of faith. It has been such an honor to have been by your side as a Spiritual mother, mentor, and mandated Intercessor!

I want to encourage you once again to keep pressing, and most of all, do not ever give up! Simply surrender to the purposes and plans of God for your life. Since the day I met you, I have known God has a mandate on your life, and the enemy is trying everything to abort it. I pray you will allow God to AWAKEN you!

Ephesians 1:18 "I pray that the eyes of your heart may be enlightened in order that you may know the hope to which he has called you, the riches of his glorious inheritance in his holy people."

Psalm 139:13-17 "For you created my inmost being, you knit me together in my mother's womb. I praise you because I am fearfully and wonderfully made, Your works are wonderful, I know that full well. My frame was not hidden from you when I was made in the secret place when I was woven together in the depths of the earth. Your eyes saw my unformed body; all the days ordained for me were written in your book before one of them came to be. How precious to me are your thoughts, God! How vast is the sum of them!"

Acknowledgments

I want to give honor where honor is due, which is first and foremost to my Abba Father God, my Lord, and Savior Jesus Christ. Thank you for the Mandate and Gifts you have entrusted to me for your PURPOSE!

I would also like to acknowledge my husband Teumalo for walking hand in hand with me on this journey, and you have been so patient and such an encouragement to me. Your support, creativity, and love have been amazing, and I thank God for you! You have pushed and mentored me as I birth out the purposes and promises of God with this book.

I acknowledge my wonderful children Bryan, Devin, and Hayley, God's greatest gifts to me! I am so thankful for the purposes and callings on each of your lives!

To my great Anointed Mentors, Apostle Robert Dowell, you have given me so much wisdom over the years. You have believed in me even when I did not believe in myself. You have been a great teacher, pastor, Spiritual father, and mentor. Thank you for giving me the tools to birth out this God-mandated book that will inspire and encourage many.

Bishop Ilinda Jackson, one of the most anointed women of God, was placed in my life. We have done so much ministry together, and it was God-ordained! Thank you for pushing me into my call and allowing me room to bring my portion on many occasions. You have been a wonderful example in my life over the years! You have been a great mentor, spiritual mother, and wonderful friend to have alongside me in this journey! I love you dearly.

I have had many other great Anointed Men and Women of God like Apostle Kim Wayne Shahan that have poured and imparted into my life over the years, and I am thankful for each of them as they pressed me into the Mandate on my life!

Introduction

Women, we are created with purpose and Destiny! I want to encourage you as you begin to venture into reading and meditate on the Chapters of this book that we will discuss the ups and down, the highs and the lows of fulfilling your God-given Purpose! I believe if your eye has caught this book, it is because there is a yearning somewhere within you to know why you were created and what your **PURPOSE** is. Why are you here, and what is it that will help you fulfill your dreams and inspirations to be satisfied even when you are in a season where nothing appears to be going right when things do not appear to make sense, and everything seems broken or lost or at a standstill. I desire to help expand your thinking and deposit something great within you, and that is God-given purpose. **PURPOSE** lets you know that when things appear wrong or out of place in your life's situation or circumstances, that purpose will keep you pressing even in the toughest of times! Even when life has, you backed up against a corner. *Purpose* will help you find a way out!

I will be the first to say that this journey has been wonderful and intense, and complex. But during life's issues, the one thing that has kept me going is *purpose*. However, I will talk about where I may have set purpose aside at times in some seasons or left her behind. We will talk about when we were confident and doing our best and when we appear to be successful and when we were at our low and appear to be insecure and wonder if we even fit or have a purpose anymore. This book will explore all the possibilities of fulfilling your God-given Purpose and living in such a way that will bless you as well as bless others. You will even be inspired to help pull other women up and out of the mire so that they can be a woman of purpose and a woman of influence. So let me encourage you now before you decide that it is not for you! Or how could you possibly ever be that woman of purpose because of your past or even maybe your present? Journey with me and allow God to touch You and show you why you are that woman of *purpose* with great potential.

His first purpose and desire are that you be born into a relationship with Him, Jesus Christ. I want to encourage you if you do not know him or have a relationship with Him; that is where purpose will begin! You were created to know him. So let me invite you to say a simple prayer that you may come to know the designer of your God-given purpose! The one that knows everything about you, even before the foundations of the earth.

Or maybe You need to rededicate your life back to him; pray this prayer with me out loud.

Dear Lord,

I come to you, and I confess that Jesus Christ came in the flesh and was your only begotten son, who died and was hung on a Cross for my sins. And in three days arose again! I ask that you come into my life and be my lord and savior. I give my life and dedicate it to you; I ask that you begin to unfold your plan and purpose, that you reveal your gifts to me for my life that I may follow you all day of my life with your purpose.

John 3:16 "For God so loved the world that he gave his one and only Son, that whosoever believes in him shall not perish but have eternal life."

Chapter 1

Beautifully Rooted In Christ

Jeremiah 17:7-8 NIV "But blessed is the one who trusts in the Lord, whose confidence is in him.

They will be like a tree planted by the water that sends out its roots by the stream. It does not fear when heat comes; its leaves are always green. It has no worries in a year of drought and never fails to bear fruit."

Root- The part of a plant that attaches it to the ground or to support, typically underground, conveys water and nourishment to the rest of the plant via numerous branches and fibers.

He lets us know right there when our trust and confidence are in Him, not in ourselves but in him...we will never fail to bear fruit. It is awesome that he gives us a word of encouragement that we will bear beautiful fruit in him. We need to wait patiently in our seasons and stay close to him.

Isaiah 30:15 "For thus saith, the Lord God, the Holy One of Israel: "In returning and rest shall ye be saved, in quietness and in confidence shall be your strength."

It is important for us to be rooted in the Lord, having a sure foundation in Him with a personal relationship. Our roots will go deeper by spending time getting the proper nutrients we need in his WORD, and we cannot have deep roots if we are not rooted in his word; his word is a lamp unto our feet and gives us direction for daily living.

Psalms 119:105 "Your word is a lamp for my feet, a light on my path."

His word lights our way for decisions and directives on how we should act accordingly to life's situations that may arise! Our roots go deep when we are consistent in his word, the bread of life.

Mathew 4:4 "But He answered and said, "It is written; 'Man shall not live by bread alone, but by every word that proceeds out of the mouth of God."

God knew his word would sustain us in the time of drought, and we need to stay close to the word of God and hide it in our hearts.

When we take the time to build a solid foundation in Him, we will be able to stand in the times of adversity, and adversity will come we live in a fallen world.

But with God by our side, we can maneuver our way through this journey. I have gone through many adversities in my own life, and had I not built a relationship with the Lord and discovered firsthand his faithfulness and how he has always kept me, I would not be here today. I cannot even imagine a life without him. The way you can develop stronger roots and a strong relationship with him is first and foremost getting to know him; if you do not know him, you will not understand him. So, over the years, I have taken the time to go deep with him, through times of mediation on his word, spending intimate time in his presence, evaluating my life, and offering repentance of those things known and unknown, worshiping him in adoration and reverence. And most of all, surrendering to his will as much as possible, living a life of obedience. It does not mean we are perfect by any means; we will miss the mark at times, but when we want to please the Lord, our roots cannot help but go deep in a relationship with him, a loving father.

We will all have times where we feel we are dried up, life may seem at a pause, and nothing seems to be going right; these are the times our roots will keep us steadfast, immovable in him. We do not need to be ashamed when we experience times like these and everyone has them let me assure you. Instead, these are the times we need to lean into him even more and trust what we know about him, his faithfulness, his gentleness, his mercy, and grace.

2 Corinthians 12:9 But he said to me, "My grace is sufficient for you, for my power is made perfect in weakness. "Therefore, I will boast more gladly about my weaknesses so that Christ's power may rest on me. That is why, for Christ's sake, I delight in weaknesses, in insults, in hardships, in persecutions, in difficulties."

I had a hard season that was one of my darkest hours. Now that I look back and see how my life still blossomed after the darkness and how things can still grow after a season of darkness in your life, the darkness today I found gives me a greater understanding today of the grace of God that was in my life to get me through that season. But not only did it get me through, but it also made me that more thankful for all the times I spent building my relationship with the Lord and allowing my roots to go deep so that when I hit that dark season, my roots kept me attached to the father. And I made it through that season of drought. So, I have a better understanding today of how deep my roots go.

Those roots do not come up so easy during the storms of life; the roots may get bruised or stretched, or even malnourished dry and become tender, but they go deep into the father's love.

Isn't it good to know that he understands our weaknesses, he understands we are human and not perfect? That in our despair, in our weaknesses, he is there offering us a beautiful thing called grace.

When you are rooted and the storms of life come, you will not be easily tossed to and fro. So let me encourage you that seasons of drought in our lives do not last forever, just like seasons in the natural, the season will change, and things will begin to bloom and blossom in your life again!

The seeds you have planted in seasons past may seem dormant or like nothing is coming forth but continue to water and nurture yourself in the word and in his presence, and your season of drought will soon be over, and before you know it, you will begin to see new life.

Isaiah 43:19 "See, I am doing a new thing! Now it springs up; do you not perceive it? I am making a way in the wilderness and streams in the wasteland."

I will talk more about seasons and some of the things we go through in the upcoming chapters, and that when we surrender in every season, God will make a way in the wilderness just like he said he would.

Proverbs: 3:5-6 "Trust in the Lord with all your heart and lean not on your own understanding; in all your ways submit to him, and he will make your paths straight."

Time to *REFLECT*:

What is your desire in this moment and season of your life? Are you in a dry season or a Blooming season? What would you like the Lord to do in this season of your life? Meditate on what you can do to allow your roots to be nourished and strengthened.

_____

_____

_____

_____

_____

_____

_____

_____

John 7:38 "Whoever believes in me, as the Scripture has said, out of his heart will flow rivers of living water."

Chapter 2

Purpose

Since the foundations of the earth, God spoke your name into existence, and he had a great desire for you to fulfill your purpose here on earth. He did now want you walking around aimlessly with no hope. He wanted you to know that even in your darkest hour, he is with you and grants your purpose. He wants to be the one to fulfill the void within you! He is your counselor, comforter, and your best friend.

Psalms 8:4 states, "What is a man that you are mindful of him."

In Psalms 139, it states that God knew you; he knows everything about YOU. He knows when you are up and when you are down. He knows when you lie down in your bed or when you are in your darkest hour, God says he is still there with you! He states he knew you even as you were formed in your mother's womb, and you may be even thinking that you are a mistake, maybe your parents did not want you, possibly even considered abortion. But God wanted you and desired you! You are not here by chance, and you are not here because you are a mistake, you are fearfully and wonderfully made, and all your days were written, yet there were none of them! So why have you possibly had so much hell in your life up to this point? Why does it appear others are passing you by? Purpose and Destiny unfold as you desire them and yield to them and pursue them. You cannot live without them, and there is something in you that keeps crying out for more, Lord I need understanding, insight into your plan for my life. As we seek him, he will reveal to us his master plan! God wants you to ask him what he has for you or desires for your life.

Mathew 7:7 "Ask, and it will be given to you; seek, and you will find; knock, and it will be opened for you. For everyone who asks receives, and he who seeks finds, and to him who knocks it will be opened."

Purpose drives life instead of the world driving you. Purpose encourages, inspires, and births vision and hope for your life. It helps you to reach your dreams to go further than you ever even thought possible. Purpose keeps your heart beating and going in life so that you have reason to live. Purpose gets you motivated and keeps you moving! Vision for your life will keep you pressing even when times get difficult. Something about the purpose drives us inwardly; could it be because we were created for a purpose? Purpose will cause us to go the extra mile; it will cause us to press when we did not know if there was anything left within us. Purpose will make us do things we never thought possible; as we yield to purpose, we begin to see the manifestation of God's purpose yielding beautiful fruit within our lives, home, ministries, relationships, and jobs.

The more you see vision and purpose coming to pass, the more inspired you are to keep pressing and gain new and higher heights!

You become stronger and more confident in who you are and what you were created for. You begin to sense your Kingdom identity in Him and truly start to live again.

When vision dies or appears to be dead, somehow it always yields new hope, new direction, new insight, and new motivation. With God, there is never an end, just a new beginning!

Hebrews 12:2 "Looking unto Jesus the author and finisher of our faith."

If your dreams or your visions appear to be dead, trust me, there is a new beginning to your story just around the horizon. God loves to create; it is what he does.

There have been many times in my own life where I have thought for sure vision died; how could I press on? But God has always been faithful to continue my story and birth new hope and new vision at every end. I see that purpose is stronger than you think; it will carry you when you cannot even carry yourself. The true purpose is birthed out of a relationship with God when you come to a place in life where you know you are living to do your best to please him or be an expression of who he is in your life and the earth.

What exactly does passion do for you? First, it births expression, and it is a powerful emotion or enthusiasm. Second, it gives passionate character to something. Third, it is the object of such love or desire.

Passionate about what you do and who you are in Him. Passion and purpose go hand in hand. *The purpose* is a focus; aim, drive, and passion are the fuel that keeps you going!

Passions are what keeps you stirred up inside keeps you hopeful and joyful.

2 Timothy 1:9 "Who has saved us and called us to a holy calling, not according to our works, but according to His own purpose and Grace, which was given to us in Christ Jesus before time began."

That is why purpose lives in each one of us; we only need to discover it. What you do is not insignificant but incredibly significant to the kingdom of God and others. When you do it unto the Lord, it is your reasonable service. He has given you the grace and ability, and potential to fulfill his desire for your life. Not according to your works but according to his purpose!

What you do, instead it is in your work, career, vocation, or being a homemaker, can still all be a part of your purpose in who you were called and you are created to be. God looks at your character, gifts, talents, and all that you are made of. He sees the great potential that needs to be unlocked in each one of us. So do not think your area of influence does not matter. God can and will use you if you avail yourself to him! So just start where you are at with what you have.

Zechariah 4:10 "Do not despise the day of small beginnings."

Keep the passion alive by talking about it, visualize your dream, and set goals. Passion will only birth more passion when it stays stirred up.

How can purpose be inspired?

❖ Write about it

❖ Talk about it

❖ Share it

❖ Visualize it

❖ Be with like-minded people

❖ Attend seminars, conferences, Read books, ECT...

Habakkuk 2:2-3 "Write the vision and make it plain on tablets that he may run who reads it. For the vision is yet for an appointed time. But in the end, it will speak, and it will not lie. Therefore, though it tarries, wait for it: Because it will surely come, it will not tarry."

Tarry means to delay or to linger in expectation.

Sometimes we grow wary in our waiting! But, God knew we would have times like these; that is why it is important to keep your goals, dreams, and aspirations before you.

When you talk about your dreams and your desire, you keep yourself stirred up. This is because you are holding that fire burning within you for your heart's desire.

When you take the time to share what is in your heart with others, your plans, and your ideas, others can help celebrate your dreams and aspirations with you, challenging you to press after those dreams and visions, helping you to believe in yourself, even when times get complicated because they will.

Visualize your dream; visualize what you believe in. See yourself walking in it, attaining that dream, goal, or achievement. When you keep it before you, it will be harder to let it go or die out. See yourself accomplishing and fulfilling your dream. See yourself walking in your purpose daily, one step at a time. When you can see it, it helps you to keep it within reach as you continue to focus and meditate until you see results.

Be with like-minded people, be around, and with those that carry the same passions and desires you do. So, you can stir and feed one another. Others that are going after the same thing will help flame your fire! Spend time sharing ideas, looking or searching for the goal or dream out. Have lunch or coffee and inspire one another. Provoke one another and challenge one another to continue to press into that desire.

Mentors and successors are great people to have around to ignite and challenge you on your journey.

I have had some great mentors and Apostolic leaders to help press what was in me out of me. Even though times got difficult and challenging, they inspired me to stretch beyond my doubts and limits of what I thought I could or could not accomplish. They helped challenge me to what God had purposed for me. Have you ever noticed that others can usually see the potential you carry that you cannot see within yourself at times? I could not be where I am now, and this book indeed would not have been birthed had it not been for Godly men and women in my life encouraging me into my God-given purpose! I am forever grateful for them! When you are living in your passion, others will see that within you!

Attend seminars and conferences, read books that inspire and motivate you. Another especially important tool is to attend workshops or conferences that are already doing what you desire to do. Look and watch those that have been successful in fulfilling their dreams or living out their purpose. Ask questions and glean from the wisdom that your successors hold. Add it and write it to your vision so you can ponder when you go back and look at your dream statement. Books are a great tool to inspire, and they give keys to wisdom. Books that are in line with your passion will help keep the vision before you, as you are inspired by others that have gone before you and have blazed the trail!

A lot of women do not feel they have a purpose within. Therefore, they do not really find an inspired, fulfilling life within themselves or who they are individually. We all struggle in some areas of self-worth, so I am here to encourage you to give purpose a try. Aim for something you never thought you could do, yet you could never quite let go. No matter how hard you have tried to let that thing or thought, or desire go, it just keeps coming back around to you. And the more you talk about it, the more you realize you still have not let go. That means it is still alive within you for a reason. It may be hard work at times or even quite uncomfortable.

The purpose will challenge you; it will stretch you beyond measure, reaching for and grabbing for the very thing you thought was impossible.

Luke 1:37 "For with God, nothing will be impossible."

Purpose and passion must be honest. It must be birthed out of who you are. Not someone else. You are not a copy of someone else; you were created to be an original. Take time to look and search within, what your creator has placed within you, what you are good at, and what you enjoy doing. What do you do that blesses you as well as others? Use this to make a difference and be an influence wherever you are.

Nehemiah 8:10 "For the joy of the Lord is my strength."

Psalms 27:13 "I would have lost heart unless I had believed, that I would see the goodness of the Lord in the land of the living."

The story of Jeremiah in chapter 1 shares how he was called since the foundations of the earth, that God had called him as he was even in his mother's womb. God knew what Jeremiah would one day be in the Kingdom as well as what he would do. God also knew Jeremiah wanted to run from the voice and call of God! When Jeremiah yielded to the voice and instructions of the Lord, then he was able to walk out his purpose and what he was created for. Jeremiah was ordained by God, not by man but by God. God will use men or women to validate or assure the call they see on your life. But it is then up to us to respond. Jeremiah was called to be separate from many others because he was called to make a difference in his area of influence that God had called him to. Jeremiah's function was to be a prophet in the Kingdom, which was his true spiritual identity. As he learned to step into his function, he was then able to fulfill his purpose.

What has God ordained for your life? There are so many possibilities that lie within you when you yield to God and as you press your way to seek and search for purpose.

Time to **REFLECT:** What do you believe God has placed in your hands to use to encourage and bless others? What are a few qualities you like about yourself? What would you like God to reveal to you this season about who you are in Him? What would you want him to reaffirm in you!

_____

_____

_____

_____

_____

2 Timothy 1:9 "Who hath saved us and called us with a holy calling, not according to our works, but in accordance with His own purpose and grace, which was given to us in Christ Jesus before the world began."

Chapter 3

Who Am I

Who am I is a question at one point or another in our life's that we have probably all asked ourselves? Who am I, what am I here for, and what is my purpose in life?

Your creator has all those answers for you, and He is waiting to unveil your purpose one step at a time as you trust him to lead you even when you do not understand things that go on or happen in your life. He will be your greatest encourager to cheer you on as you press your way to have a fulfilling life.

The Lord desires that you would be enlightened and that your eyes (spiritual eyes) may be opened. For you to perceive and see what God sees? God sees the great potential within you, and he longs to help you bring it out!

Ephesians 1:18 "I pray that the eyes of your heart may be enlightened in order that you may know the hope to which he has called you, the riches of his glorious inheritance in his holy people."

The more we began to embrace ourselves, the more we will embrace what lies within us and before us. And the more we will discover who we are! We will then begin to get excited about our journey with our creator, knowing that he cares for us, placing great gifts within each one of us, waiting for us to open them up so we can begin to bloom and blossom wherever we are.

Jeremiah 29:11 "For I know the thought that I think toward you says the Lord, thoughts of peace and not of evil, to give you a future and a hope."

He wants you to understand the investment He has placed within you!

An investment is something worth paying the price for; it may be profitable or useful in the future.

God desires all of you! He sees more in you than you could ever see in yourself.

EPHESIANS 3:20 "Now to Him who is able to do exceedingly abundantly above all that we ask or think, according to the power that works in us."

Who are you in the Kingdom is the first thing you need to realize; you are here on earth to be about your father's business? First, we must realize that we are not true citizens here; our time here is but for a moment. You were born into God's kingdom. We are ambassadors and disciples of Jesus Christ.

What is your true Spiritual Identity!

If you love to teach, then teach; if you love to be a mother, then be a mother, do it with the best of your ability as unto the Lord, and he will do the rest. Be an influence wherever you are.

If there is a dream or vision within you, begin to live and breathe your Kingdom purpose and identity until it is manifested. Begin where you are with what you have until it becomes who you are!

WHO AM I

What is your passion in the Kingdom: begin to give expression to it? I love to teach, preach and evangelize the word of God.

I am an EXPRESSION of who God is in my life:

Acts 17:28 "For in Him we live and move and have our being, as also some of your poets have said, we are also His offspring."

It is in your spiritual DNA, you are His offspring; just like it is natural with your children, they have your DNA; they have your bloodline running through them. So, they have some of your genes!

They are a representation of who you are. There is a part of you in your children, which is why they look like you or the father. That is why some have more dominant features or characteristic traits. We need to rise and be who God says we are in the Kingdom! He has always known your spiritual identity and function in the Kingdom because you are His child. Therefore you are a product of His DNA, and you came from Him! You are fashioned after His likeness; you are His offspring!

EXPRESSION: The act of Expressing or conveying a manifestation of something that expresses and communicates. An outward manifestation of disposition. Something that symbolizes something else.

You are an *Expression* of a heavenly language from a heavenly Kingdom!

GOD IS THE CREATOR

I AM THE CREATED

TOGETHER GOD AND I ARE CREATIVE

I am an ambassador of my father's Kingdom or estate; I rule and reign with a certain function in His Kingdom. I represent His Kingdom!

- ❖ His Authority

- ❖ His Domain

- ❖ His leadership

WHO AM I: I am anointed and appointed by God almighty!

I am an expression of who He is in me: I express God's beauty through my creativity and expression of what I do. I am passionate about what I do because my God is passionate about me!

WHO AM I?

Mother, wife, friend, teacher, pastor?

Christ was the ultimate everything, and you are one in the same. GOD IS IN YOU!

Start where you are and begin to be an expression of God in your area of influence, your home, work, marriage, or Ministry.

WHO AM I-BE WHO GOD HAS CALLED YOU TO BE IN HIS

KINGDOM! Walk in your true spiritual identity!

Not the identity the world tries to put on you!

If you are a prophet, prophesy and do it unto God! Do it with the ability and grace that God has given you for now. (Prophesy encouragement, he desires all to prophesy) If you teach, do it with the grace that God has given you! If you are a wife, be the best wife you can be. There is always improvement that can be made wherever were at and in whatever were doing.

Eph 4:7,11 "But to each one of us GRACE was given according to the measure of Christ's gift. And He himself gave some to be Apostles, Prophets, Evangelists and some Pastors and Teachers for the equipping of the saints for the work of the MINISTRY for the edifying of the body of Christ."

This is expressed to those that feel they are called to the fivefold ministry; he desires and needs each of us to do our part and to edify one another in our perspective area.

Equipping is making fit, preparing, and training qualified for service. Adjustments so the church will not be out of joint; we each represent a part of the church.

WHO AM I-I am a product of the goodness of God in my life? I could not even be doing what I am doing without the Grace of God upon my life! But also, being confident in your identity.

Romans 8:19-22 "For the earnest expectation of the creation eagerly waits for the revealing or manifestation of the sons and daughters of God to be revealed. For whom He foreknew He also predestined to be conformed to the image of His Son, the firstborn amongst the brethren, moreover whom He predestined these He called. Whom He called He also justified and whom He justified He also glorified."

He knew you would be revealed at an appointed time, and He foreknew you. He had knowledge of you because He is your creator! He predestined you, He decreed, He foreordained you by divine will, and He needs for you to agree with him! He chose you; you have been selected by God himself and favored by God!

So go and produce and help reproduce for the Kingdom, impart unto others, disciple and help raise up and encourage others into the Kingdom of God! Use what God has given you to express God's love and beauty of creation to others! It is not about you! It is about EXPRESSING ANOTHER KINGDOM. There is always someone else that needs to hear your message of what you have conquered in life. There is always someone a little lower than where you may be in life and needs your encouragement.

You are a demonstration of the Kingdom of God working in and through you!

Philippians 1:6 "Being confident of this very thing, that He who has begun a good work in you will complete it until the day of Jesus Christ."

All creation is groaning, waiting, longing, yearning earnestly waiting for you to step into your Kingdom Identity and be revealed in the earth.

See, the Kingdom already knows your Identity because it was

created and purposed since the earth's foundations! Creation is waiting for you to be manifested and revealed with power and authority and demonstration of the Kingdom of God!

Creation is waiting for you to rule and reign and to bring back into order some things, to declare and decree that it may be established in the earth, to bind and loose, and heal and restore.

See, you have been created with purpose and Destiny to be fulfilled in the earth right now; you are in the right time frame of God for your life. It is now that the sons and daughters of God are to rise and manifest themselves it's now!

Galatians 1:15-16 "But when it pleased God, who separated me from my mother's womb and called me through His grace."

The story of Paul also describes how he was separated from his mother's womb and called according through Grace. He was called by God through grace to one day reveal Jesus Christ into the earth realm. You also are called through grace that you would reveal his son through who you are. We all have a mess, and we all have a message in Christ through grace.

God is such a diverse God; that is why we are such a diverse people. God has invested you with his Kingship and his authority.

Ordain is to establish by appointment, decreed over your life, to invest with priestly authority!

There are many DIVERSITIES BECAUSE GOD IS SO CREATIVE

❖ Many different functions

❖ Many different callings

❖ Many different gifts

❖ Many different ministries

1 Corinthians 12:4 "There are diversities of gifts but the same spirit: there are differences of MINISTRIES (Areas of influence) but the same Lord. And there are diversities of ACTIVITIES but the same God who works all in all. But the manifestation of the Spirit is given to each one for the profit of all. UNITY and for the encouragement of others and the uplifting and building of the saints of God!"

Stay in your ELEMENT, focus on your God-given strengths and let God work on your weaknesses. Operate in the grace God has supplied for you. God will provide you with growth and EXPANSION when your obedient to do what he has already beckoned, and unction's you to do. Do not worry about what you cannot do; start with what you can.

God does not call the equipped; He equips the call.

He will train you as you continue to say yes and are submitted to the Call and be who He has called you to be in Him and through Him! You are a revealer of who He is in and through you!

Generals: Are your leaders they go and help blaze the way for you so you can be trained up and begin to function in your gifting and your call; they are the forerunners that go before you!

We must learn to get back into proper formation; when you operate in your God-given function, every joint is fitted and fastened together so that we begin to march to the clarion call as a body in FILE, RANK, AND ORDER!

An Army is not supposed to be out of order or out of sync, especially when they are supposed to be marching together in war! Everyone has their rank, their job, their call of duty, and their area of influence! Be an influence where God has called you or wherever you are at this moment or season in your life. We can all take ground for the sake of the Kingdom if we all do our part.

Eph 4:16 "From whom the whole body joined and knitted together by what every joint(function) supply, according to the effective working by which every part does its share causes growth of the body for edifying of itself in love."

He is trying to be an expression to you and through you! He is passionate about you! He is expressing Himself to you through this book that you would begin to step into your identity!

Time to **REFLECT:** Are you struggling with the purposes of God for your life? Are you wondering why you are here? Ask God WHO AM I? Let him begin to affirm you in his unconditional love for you and His desire for you!

_____

_____

_____

_____

_____

_____

_____

_____

Psalm 139:14 *"I praise you because I am fearfully and wonderfully made; your works are wonderful; I know that full well."*

Chapter 4

Identity Crisis

So many times, we struggle with our God-given purpose because we struggle with our identity. We struggle with the fact that we are unique in our way, different from others, and most of all, there is only one you and one of me! We are diverse in our ways, and yet we struggle with how God created us. We focus more on our inabilities. Most of this comes from where we were born and our family history. How we were raised, and of course, our life's situations and circumstances have all played a vital part, good or bad, in whom we have become.

Therefore, instead of embracing ourselves, we shun the idea that we are different, where and how we fit. We, as God's women, need to come to a place where we are renewed by the transformation of our minds!

Romans 12:2 "And do not be conformed to this world, but be transformed by the renewing of your mind, that you may prove what is that good and acceptable and perfect will of God."

We are not being conformed to this world. The world has tried to shape us and tell us what we were not, but our gracious creator is trying to tell us who we are! When we gave our life to Christ, the world did not have the final say; HE DID! He stated behold in **2 Corinthians 17 "Therefore, if anyone is in Christ, he is a new creation, old things have passed away, behold, all things have become new."** you are now in Him. He wants and desires to establish a new identity in you.

Romans 8:29 "For whom He foreknew, He also predestined to be conformed to the image of His Son."

This happens daily as we yield to Him and discover our purpose and identity in our very own creator.

He wants to take you from the old identity to your new identity in him. His identity will amaze you, astound you and excite you! It is like getting a whole new makeover from who and what you thought you were to whom he declares you are. Get ready to be changed and renewed in your new God-given Identity.

- ❖ You will learn to break old habits.
- ❖ Old cycles
- ❖ Old concepts
- ❖ And break generational and ancestral curses passed down.

Let us look at what causes an Identity Crisis? Past hurts or tragedy, crisis, or major transitions. It brings about insecurity and misunderstanding at the way we perceive things!

Testimony: Because of my past hurts, the physical abuse, the emotional abuse, rejection, being violated taught me that I did not fit in and told me I would never amount to anything. I was a failure! *I believed the lie; the lie still tries to control and dictate my future at times... I got stuck in a false identity* I had a hard time moving forward and into my future. A bad relationship is all I knew. My life began to spiral downward into attempts of suicide at a young age! False identity will even try to kill you at times.

Finally, my mess became my MESSAGE.

My pain helped shape me into who I am today! I did not like or ask for it, and it is what it is. It just happened! But now I know I do not want to go back to that lie!

Identity Crises are a psychosocial state or condition of disorientation and roles of confusion occurring, especially due to conflict internally and externally, that can be caused by bad experiences, pressures, or expectations and can produce anxiety about self and life!

We conflict within ourselves because we do not like what we see or feel.

What false Identity produces... Bad habits are learned behaviors of protecting ourselves. We try to fix it rather than dealing with what is going on internally! Even if it is not suitable for us, we do it anyway, and it causes us even more pain! We are finding ways to self-medicate our deep hurts, and it could be drugs, alcohol, pornography, gambling, to name a few.

Anxiety is a form of fear that is produced because were afraid to look within and out.

A bad motive or habit does not mean our heart is necessarily wrong;

we just learned to do things and react the wrong way. Wrong thought patterns about ourselves.

What do you do to get out of the Identity crisis?

One day at a time, work on the way you see yourself, start within.

Look and focus on your good attributes, your strengths.

Love and forgive yourself and others.

Forgiving yourself, that's the hardest.

Focus on the possibilities ahead of yourself.

Pay attention to your needs, treat yourself well, your worth it. We all need affirmation and love; we were created for these things. Do not be so hard on yourself if you fall or fail; get back up and try again. Failure is giving up; success is when you keep trying to move forward and continue to make progress. When you can look back and see you are not in the same place you were before, it means you have made progress to step into a new identity and breaking the cycles of yesterday's pain.

Think about it for a minute; what could happen if there was a change? What could happen if you began to believe the opposite of the lies?

We take on the identity of what others have told us or deemed us to be. We believe the lies that things will not change for us, that this is just the way it is.

You do not believe you're worth better, so you go back to what you have been told or what you are familiar with. The world tries to put on us lies, rejection, pain, abandonment, and indifference and that we are the least of them and do not fit.

Self-perception then leads to self-deception! Believing a lie about ourselves! Self-Sabotage releases us from taking responsibility for ourselves. It is easier for us to blame everyone else and everything else. This is the self-abuse we then project onto ourselves. When we see ourselves a certain way, it is hard to move forward or even think positively or let alone see possibilities that lie within. We must take one step at a time.

You wake up one day, and you wonder how you ever got here, where you are at. You never intended things to go this far or get this out of control. Then, you have an awakening and realize things need to be different.

What are the possibilities for your new identity?

Where you could be if you focused

What you could be doing

Starting where you are with what you have

Boundaries that are healthy but not unrealistic

Goals you know will stretch you but that you can accomplish, that will cause change

We tend to get stuck in our failures; we focus on our weaknesses versus our strengths!

Because of our past or present pain, we are afraid to move forward or become very hesitant and procrastinate. It is hard to look at tomorrow, let alone the future. If we do not know our identity today, how could we possibly know our identity for tomorrow?

Our internal pain though not pleasant, can push us forward if we allow it, we get fed up with the mundane of life just barely getting by, we gain courage instead of I cannot we now say I can! Fear is always telling you what you are not. Fear will hold you down, and you must face your fears! Sometimes we even try to keep and hold on to the lies and hurts of pain because we do not know how to let go and break the chains we're use too.

The greatest lie we are told is that we will never amount to anything or anyone. I dare you to believe something different. I had to be willing to press past my pain and move forward if I desired to see change. I had to press past my fears, even fears of failure.

I look at where I was to where I am in my new identity; Grace helped me become who I am today, a minister, a mother, wife, and good friend and spiritual mother and mentor to many, passionate in life even though times get tough still. I never had a reason to live. Now I want to live and am passionate about life. If I had never taken the steps, I would not be where I am today!

Not perfect; you just need progress.

How bad do you want the dream within you to live? How bad do you want to change in your situation or circumstances? You must keep pressing one step at a time. It is not easy, but it is worth it!

Identity: Is the distinct personality of an individual regarded as a persisting entity. Individuality. What separates and distinguishes us from others. We all have something unique about us and something to offer. "We are fearfully and wonderfully made."

What is your identity? I had to take my masks off to gain a new identity with every new season in my life, and as I did, I gained and am still gaining individuality which is identity! Sometimes we do not even realize when we have picked back up the mask and scars of yesterday's pains at times, but when we pick back up the masks of the old ways of doing things, we must instantly take them back off.

What great things lie within you that you yet need to discover?

I dare you to believe within and challenge yourself to gain a new and greater identity even with your struggles, weaknesses and allow grace to carry you to places you never thought possible. Be inspired to press into greater vision and newer heights than ever before as you allow purpose to be birthed in the identity of who you are and were created to be, you are an original, and the world needs you!

Time to **REFLECT:** What causes you to struggle with your Identity? What hardships have you encountered that may have affected how you see yourself? Ask God to bring healing to those areas.

_____

_____

_____

_____

_____

_____

_____

_____

Genesis 1:27 "So God created mankind in His own image, He created them male and female He created them."

Chapter 5

The Strength of a Woman

Women, when they put their mind to it, are always able to focus and press into what it is they want. There is endurance and Strength about women that when times get difficult, they can hold on and hang in there. They can concentrate on what needs to get done, and they just do it!

It is just like that of a pregnant woman; she endures nine months of transition within her body physically and emotionally. Then when the appointed time comes and it will, she has no choice but to push and birth that child out. She musters up the last bit of strength and, with all she has, pushes past the pain and presses the new birth out. She then no longer remembers the pain because the joy is here.

Even in the most extreme pain were able to endure it and bear down and push through it!

Philippians 4:13 "I can do all things through Christ who strengthens me."

Strengthen: "Make strong or stronger, reinforced in giving added strength and support, the act of increasing the strength of something. To strengthen in authority, to strengthen in obligation."

An obligation is the same as a commitment; it is a duty or course of action, the state of being obligated to do something. A personal relation to whom one is indebted, something for service or favor.

We are indebted to our relationship with Christ to fulfill our God-given Destiny and purposes for the sake of the Kingdom!

In every area and every circumstance, it is the willingness to allow Christ's power to sustain us in difficulty and scarcity.

When I am weak, he is strong... So, we learn to yield to his grace so we can gain his strength.

2 Corinthians 12:9 "And He said my grace is sufficient for you, my strength is made perfect in weakness. Therefore, most gladly, I will rather boast in my infirmities that the power of Christ may rest upon me."

The Lord said there is something about the *strength* of a woman he has placed within each of us; though we are frail and sometimes appear weak, we are extraordinarily strong and resilient.

Strength: Is the quality or state of being strong. Ability to bear things, Capacity for exertion or endurance, Intellectual, vigor, power, as strength of judgment. Power of resisting attacks. Something or someone that gives one strength or is a source of encouragement.

Women of God have the inner *strength* of beauty, and their outer appearance is confidence.

Not that we walk in pride or arrogance, but we have learned to walk in a soft, quiet trust in the Lord that makes one confident.

Isaiah 30:15 "In confidence and quietness shall be your strength."

She lifts her head high in having confidence in her relationship with the Lord; she is confident in knowing she does not have to be perfect or right, but her confidence in knowing that the Lord will do what he said he would do, that he would perform his word on her behalf. She knows he is for her and not against her, and this gives her the reassurance she needs to press through every circumstance, knowing He is her rearguard!

Isaiah 41:10 "Fear not I am with you: be not dismayed, for I am your God, I will strengthen you; Yes, I will help you. I will uphold you with my righteous right hand."

He will harden you to difficulties. He is your rearguard.

Everything the enemy throws at you will become a mere agitation to you. You will learn to set your face like flint.

Isaiah 50:7 "For the Lord God will help me: Therefore, I will not be disgraced: Therefore, I have set my face like a flint, and I know that I will not be ashamed."

Breaking down the meaning of Strengthen

Strong-Proverbs 31:17 *"She girds herself with strength. And strengthens her arms."*

Strength and honor are in her clothing. (She knows that she is in right standing with God.) She strengthens her arms by praising the Lord.

She encourages herself in her inner man by praying and worshiping, being drawn into an intimate place in the Lord. She understands what the heartbeat of the Lord is for her because she learns to yield in a place of intimacy with her creator; the lover of her should be the source of her strength. Therefore, she encourages herself in his presence.

Women are full of tenacity when they need to be, and they are persistent. Therefore, we need to use this tenacity as a determination toward our purpose.

James 5:16 "The fervent prayer of a righteous man availed much."

Strong women also learn to reverence God in their lives; they have a profound respect for Him.

Proverbs 31:10 "But a woman who fears the Lord, she shall be praised."

She respects the Lord and His ways; she submits herself to quick obedience rather than sacrifices. She does what is pleasing to the Lord.

Women have Endurance which is the power to withstand hardship or stress.

1 Corinthians 13:7 "Bears all things, believes all things, hopes all things, and endures all things."

She can bear down and press and push against hardship. She believes in the call upon her life; therefore, she is focused and aims toward the high calling in Christ.

Philippians 3:12 "Not that I have already attained or am already perfected, but I press on, that I may lay hold of that for which Christ Jesus has also laid hold of me. Brethren, I do not count myself to have apprehended; but one thing I do forgetting those things which are behind and reaching forward to those things which are ahead. I press toward the goal for the prize of the upward call of God in Christ Jesus."

She learns to navigate and follow a planned course. She looks at life's circumstances and pursues the best route or action to take.

Ephesians 1:18 "That the eyes of your understanding would be enlightened (Wisdom) that you may know the Hope of your calling." (Course) Purpose and Destiny.

She trusts the course the Lord has set her on and follows his lead, and she is confident that he will make a way of escape for any snare the enemy has set up.

She has the act of giving; she gives of her time and resources what God has blessed her with. She is a woman of strength that gives generously to others in need to help encourage them on the path of righteousness for the Kingdom of God!

2 Corinthians 9:6 "But I say he who sows sparingly will also reap sparingly. And he who sows bountifully will also reap bountifully. So let each one give as he purposes in his heart, not grudgingly of necessity, for God loves cheerful giving."

She trusts; she has confidence and faith. She trusts in God based on past experiences; she has the trait of believing. Complete confidence in a plan or purpose. Trust in a trustful relationship.

Proverbs 3:5 "Trust in the Lord with all your heart and lean not unto your own understanding: in all your ways acknowledge Him, And He shall direct your paths."

You cannot trust Him if you never discover He created you for a purpose in this time frame.

She trusts in the Lord even when she does not even trust herself. She trusts in his word and simply says as Mary did in *Luke 1:37-38, "For with God nothing will be impossible. Then Mary said, Behold the maidservant of the Lord! Let it be to me according to your word."* Most of the time, when we believe or wait, we do not know how it will happen. So we must wait and say, let it be according to me as it is according to your word and will, Lord.

She has strong hope, a general feeling that some desire will be fulfilled. Hope about the future. An expected outcome. Optimistic.

Psalm 71:15 "For you are my hope, O Lord God; you are my trust from my youth. By you, I have been upheld from birth; you are He who took me out of my mother's womb. My praise shall be continual of you."

Hebrews 11:1 "Now Faith is the evidence of things hoped for the evidence of things not seen!"

Habakkuk 2:1 "Write the vision down and make it plain that he who reads it may run with it, for though it tarry wait shall surely come, it is yet for an appointed time, but at the end, it will speak, and it will not lie. So though it tarries, wait for it. Because it will surely come, it will not tarry."

God has pr-ordained some things for you. Trust in his strength that undergirds you in each season you encounter. He is always working on your behalf.

Isaiah 40:31 "But those who wait on the Lord shall renew their strength; they shall mount up with wings like eagles. They shall run and not be weary; they shall walk and not faint."

Nehemiah 8:10 "The joy of the Lord is your strength."

Time to **REFLECT:** What are some of your greatest strengths? How can you use these strengths to be a Blessing to others or an encouragement?

_____

_____

_____

_____

_____

_____

_____

_____

Isaiah 41:10 "So do not fear, for I am with you, do not be dismayed, for I am you, God. I will strengthen you and help you; I will uphold you with my righteous right hand."

Chapter 6

God is my Rock

1 *Sam 7:12 "Then Samuel took a stone and set it up between Mizpah and Shen and called its name Ebenezer saying, "Thus far the Lord has helped us."*

How many times has GOD been our ROCK in every situation and every circumstance that comes our way?

GOD is our ROCK in every earthly battle we will incur or face.

Sometimes this journey must be one step at a time, sometimes it is all we can take, yet we can indeed look back and say God has helped us THUS FAR!

Through our difficult times, while everything around us may be shaking, GOD IS IMMOVABLE!

God knows when to move and when not to move! Emotions or circumstances do not move God; sometimes things are not good for us, or it may not be God's timing; it could be going to cause us more headaches and heartache even in the next season. No matter how bad we think we may want or desire something, God knows what is best for us. He knows exactly when to move on our behalf, and he sees us through every season of our life. He is consistently producing purpose, even during that which the enemy meant for evil, turning it around for our good.

Genesis 50:20 "But as for you, you meant evil against me; but God meant it for good, in order to bring about as it is this day, to save many people."

He is an on-time God! Although it appears he never moves according to what we would consider our time clock or time frame. How many times can you look over some of your past seasons and now thank God he Is immovable and that he did not give you everything you thought you needed or wanted? Now you look back and see how it could have caused more damage. He did not move by what you thought you needed. THE ONLY THING GOD WAS MOVED BY WAS HIS COMPASSION FOR YOU!

A *rock* means Stability, firmness, and dependability.

Sometimes, depending on the trial we are facing, we become UNSTABLE; we begin to falter in our ways and are not sure anymore about what is going on around us. Then we begin to want a quick fix because of our pain, and we grasp at anything and everything we think will take care of that need. We get impatient with ourselves and with God, but God is our only source of strength in times like these. He is our rock in moments like these, and He is our sure foundation, something we can lean on! Even when everything we thought we knew begins to shake, we begin to have an identity crisis were not even sure of who we are in the Kingdom of GOD or the Authority or position we hold with God! We become double-minded about God, we begin to doubt ourselves, and we even start to doubt what God is attempting to do in our lives in certain seasons. It does not mean we do not love God; it does not even mean we do not have faith anymore; it means our FAITH IS BEING TRIED IN THE FIRE!

When we come out of the Fire, our Faith will be greater and stronger, and we will know and see once again GOD has helped us thus far! How do we know we have lasting FAITH if we were never tried in the FIRE? We need stability in times like these; we need a Rock OF HELP, a ROCK OF HOPE, a ROCK OF STRENGTH, a rock that does not change, that is not moved because of what is going on, and we need GOD! I do not know about you, but I need some stability in my life in times like that. God is also DEPENDABLE, and He is someone we can always depend on; when we do not know who we can trust or lean on, God is dependable! Sometimes we feel out of alignment with God's plan and purposes for our lives. We feel disconnected, and we feel fractured and broken from our brothers and sisters in Christ; we feel alone. We need someone who will and is always there for us; that is why he said, he knew at the time we would be overwhelmed with life and all that goes on around us, and he said *Hebrews 13:5, "I WILL NEVER LEAVE YOU NOR FORSAKE YOU."* Others may leave you, abandon you, reject you, but he IS DEPENDABLE! HE IS YOUR STABILITY. He is even working in you and your situations of everyday life and struggles even now. He is the God that makes a way out of no way, the Rock of all possibilities.

Does that sound like our GOD, Stable, firm, and dependable?

God is our rock and has always been our rock during difficult times; because of what a rock is made of it causes it to be solid, tough, steadfast, and immovable at times; if it is a big enough rock, the more it can handle and endure. How many know GOD is big enough! *Luke 1:37 "For with God, nothing will be impossible."*

Mathew 16:18 "And upon this ROCK I will build my church." He was saying this is a sure foundation, something that is solid and hard to tear or break up, because of what it is made of. CHRIST IS OUR ROCK look at all HE HAS DONE FOR US!

Anything built upon GOD is a sure foundation. We trust God as our rock because of times in the past, and we keep in remembrance all the things he has done for us and all that he has brought us through. GOD IS IMMOVABLE, UNSTOPPABLE, AND UNCHANGEABLE! HE IS THE SAME YESTERDAY, TODAY, AND FOREVER!

We must remember that anything built upon God or Christ Jesus is a sure foundation; we can trust that God is more than able when we are not.

He knew you would have trials and tribulations, but he said he overcame them, he will help you with all that you need, His grace is more than enough. He knows everything about you, and this is a declaration over your life of God's knowledge of you and his goodness!

When Samuel took the ROCK, he placed it on the battle site. It stood as a memorial THAT GOD WAS HIS ROCK IN TIME OF BATTLE, IN TIME OF NEEDING HELP, IN TIME OF NEED FOR DELIVERANCE FROM HIS ENEMIES!

How many MEMORIALS do you have that you can revisit where

GOD has helped you and delivered you from the snare of your enemies?

How many times has GOD been your ROCK when everything around you were being shaken and falling apart! You have many ROCKS that signify GOD HAS BEEN IMMOVABLE IN YOUR LIFE, THAT HE IS YOUR STRONG POINT. HE WAS YOUR SURE FOUNDATION! HE WAS YOUR ROCK AND YOUR FORTRESS IN TIMES OF TROUBLE!!

2 Samuel 22:2 "The lord is my ROCK and my fortress, and my deliver, The GOD of my strength of whom I trust!"

Ebenezer: In Hebrew Means ROCK of HELP OR ROCK OF HOPE

The ROCK Samuel placed between Mizpah and Shen was a MONUMENTAL STONE OR MEMORIAL, a place of remembrance, a symbolic act of what GOD had done for them!

You need to revisit your memorials of what GOD has done for you in times past when things get complicated. How many times can you now look back and see how God has sustained you, brought you through your mess, and now you have even a greater message of deliverance, healing, and victory? You can now offer encouragement and wisdom to others in need.

God has given you some things to remember, some things that have happened in your life that are not easy to forget, they are things that mark some problematic seasons of your life, and these markers leave a memorial, a place of remembrance that is left in your mind. So that you can never forget what God had done for you and how he helped you so that when you face another opposition, you can remember those memorials to help you with your faith along the way to continue in this journey and take one step at a time! DON'T FORGET WHERE YOU HAVE BEEN, PAUSE AT WHERE YOU AT, AND CONTINUE TO WHERE YOU ARE GOING!

In verse 12, Samuel says, GOD has helped us thus far, and it was a sign that GOD could and surely would help them again! Do you believe God will surely help you again?

The MEMORIAL or place of remembrance signified that THEIR HELP CAME; That GOD granted the request of the one raising the stone, which was Samuel, GOD WAS SAMUELS ROCK!

How many times can you signify that God is your rock of hope and rock of help?

Mizpah and Shen looked like a place of defeat at first, getting ready to be overtaken by enemies, but turned into a place of VICTORY.

How many times in your life did you look and feel defeated? You felt there was no way out of your situation or circumstances, you thought purpose and your dreams had come to a dead-end, but GOD showed up as your rock in time of trouble!

We must recognize God's help in our life.

Psalm 94:22 "But the Lord has been my defense, And my God the Rock of my refuge."

Psalms 61:2 "Hear my cry oh GOD attend to my prayer, for the end of the earth I will cry to you! Lead me to the ROCK that is higher than I."

God hears when we cry out to him, and he shows up! How many times have your cried out to God, and He showed up!

TRUST is a sure foundation of who GOD is in our lives.

2 Samuel 22:32 "For who is GOD? Except the LORD! And who is our rock except our GOD!"

There comes a time when you must begin to praise your GOD, and you must exalt him higher than your circumstances, higher than your enemies, higher than all that is going on around you, for it says LORD LIFT ME HIGHER!

Psalm 27:5 "For in the time of trouble, He shall hide me in His pavilion, in the secret place of His tabernacle. He shall hide me! He shall set me high upon a ROCK!

Is that your cry today, Lord set me high upon a ROCK, set me higher than all that is going on, set me higher, lift me higher than my enemies, elevate me higher in you, that you would be my strength, my safe place, my sure foundation! Higher than my circumstances and situations that I may continue to walk out purpose and Destiny.

R-refuge

O-omnipresent

C-caretaker, counselor, comforter

K-keeper

2 Samuel 22:47-51 "The Lord lives, blessed by my ROCK!"

Are you glad that the Lord lives, BLESSED BE OUR ROCK!

Time to **REFLECT:** What areas do you need God as a Rock in your life? What times in your past can you recall how God made a way for you? Take time to Reflect on His goodness. What are some of your memorials, places of remembrance where God showed up!

_____

_____

_____

_____

_____

_____

_____

_____

Psalm 77:11 "I will remember the deeds of the LORD; yes, I will remember your miracles of long ago."

Chapter 7

Preparation for his kingdom

Just as the King was having women being prepared to be chosen to be his Queen, The Lord was *preparing* you before the foundations of the earth to be chosen for his kingdom.

I want to speak to you about *preparation* for His Kingdom!

Since the foundations of the earth, King Jesus *chose* you for his kingdom! In *Psalms 139:13-17*, *"For you formed my inward parts, you covered me in my mother's womb. I will praise You, for I am fearfully and wonderfully made. So marvelous are Your works, and that my soul knows very well. My frame was not hidden from You. When I was made in secret and skillfully wrought in the lowest parts of the earth. Your eyes saw my substance, being yet unformed. And in your book, they all were written. The days fashioned for me when yet there were none of them. How precious are Your thoughts to me, O God!"*

You were in his mind as you were being created for his purpose in His kingdom, *Eph 1:4 "Just as He chose us in Him before the foundation of the world, that we should be holy and without blame before Him in love. Thus, having predestined us to adoption as sons by Jesus Christ to Himself, as sons by Jesus Christ to Himself, according to the good pleasure of His will."*

His predestined plan and strategy for your life was an eternal purpose.

Redemption cries out that God loved you so much that he gave you his only begotten son that whosoever shall call upon the name of Jesus Christ shall be saved.

John 3:16 "For God so loved the world that he gave his only begotten son that whoever believes in Him Jesus Christ, should not perish but have everlasting life.

God's desire is not that you parish but have life after this life.

Just as Esther was supposed to parish because she was a Jew. And then again because she made a petition before the King. But she found favor, and she did not perish. Because she called upon the Lord and prayed, fasted, and prepared herself before she made her request.

God had a plan in John 3:16 that you would not perish but call upon him and have eternal life, which is true purpose because its eternal purpose is everlasting!

All odds were against her, and she still helped change the course of her people and nation. Strategy is all about the Lord.

His whole purpose from the beginning was salvation that all men would be saved and come into the full knowledge of Jesus Christ and his love for them. That you would know him that you would be born into relationship with him and into his kingdom to make a difference where you are for the kingdom of God. This is a true purpose; God alone gives us our true purpose.

You are not a mistake to God! God formed you even as you were in the matrix of your mother's womb; He breathed the very breath of life into you! You are precious to him, and he cares for you. It is the enemy that comes to steal and destroy all that you have.

John 10:10 "The thief does not come except to steal, and to kill, and to destroy, I have come that they may have life and that they may life and that they may have it more abundantly."

But the purpose is birthed out of the relationship with God; the more you get to know him, the more you have hope and direction for your life. God created you with purpose inside of you, and you just must discover that God-given purpose and desire.

No matter how big or small, or insignificant you may think it is, it matters to God! You are incredibly significant, and you are on his mind.

Romans 8:29 "For whom He foreknew, He also predestined to be conformed to the image of His son, that he might be the firstborn among many brethren. Moreover, whom He predestined these He also called, whom he called, these He also justified and whom He justified and these He also glorified."

Ephesians 1:11 "In Him also we have obtained an inheritance, being predestined according to the purpose of Him who works all things according to the counsel of His will."

Ephesians 2:10 "For we are His workmanship, created in Christ Jesus for good works, which God prepared beforehand that we should walk in them."

Isaiah 49:1 "Listen, O coastlands, to Me, and take heed, you peoples from afar! The Lord has called me from the womb: From the matrix of my mother, He has made mention of my name!"

The Lord continues to tell you that he makes mention of you even by your name. that you are continually upon his heart and mind, that you are important to him and his Kingdom, that he desires all of you, that he desires a relationship with you that he can give you hope, encouragement and strengthen you in the days ahead. He can give you a reason to want to live when there seems to be no reason to live in the natural. When everything is coming against you, he wants to give you the peace and hope that surpasses all your understanding, and he wants to do what you cannot do for yourself! Then you will begin to have confidence not in yourself but who you are in him because you know that he cares and loves you deep within.

Isaiah 30:15 "In quietness and confidence shall be your strength."

Jeremiah 29:11-13 "For I know the thoughts that I think toward you says the Lord, thoughts of peace and not of evil, to give you a future and a hope. Then you will go and pray to Me, and I will listen to you. And you will seek Me and find Me when you search for Me with all your heart."

The enemy is the one that plans to steal, kill and destroy all that you have.

God continues to tell you he prepared you for purpose; what is the purpose, you may ask. The purpose is a result that it is desired to obtain and is kept, action toward something. A specific intention. Serving or having a purpose! God is not a respecter of people; he will do the same for you that he did for someone else. If you will begin to do whatever you do unto the Lord and allow Him to show you how you can make a difference.

When you have a vision, you then get provision because you are now active toward something. You agree and align with God and why you were created.

Acts 17:28 "For in Him we live and move and have our being."

Habakkuk 2:1 "Write the vision and make it plain on tablets. That he may run who reads it. For the vision is yet for an appointed time. But in the end, it will speak, and it will not lie. Though it tarries, wait for it. Because it will surely come, it will not tarry! God-given desires and strategies!"

Provision involves Preparation for planning, sight, and thought.

*When you have a sense of purpose and Destiny, you have an expected outcome. Therefore, when times get complicated, and everything is coming against you. Something within you keeps you persevering and helps you to endure, because you know that you know there's purpose and destiny in your life. So it is all about your perspective and how you look at your situation. But when you have a vision, you will aim toward that vision with all you have because you know that you have somewhere to go and something to fulfill.

God used women that others probably did not see any potential in; they are cast away in men's eyes. They were considered nobodies.

I want to talk to you about another woman that was handpicked by God chosen for a specific time and purpose…

In Luke 1:28-38 …Mary was chosen by God, handpicked to reveal his glory in the earth. She found favor just like Esther in the sight of God.

She did not understand how or why God wanted to use her when he could have used anyone else. But she did not fight with the Lord. Instead, she submitted to his request just like Esther. She did what appeared to be an Unimaginable request, and she could not even wrap her natural mind around it. But in her yes, she conceived God's purposes for her life and performed one of the greatest miracles ever told!

Will, we too totally abandon ourselves to him, will we say Yes Lord be it unto me according to thy will and word.

See, Mary and Esther's confidence were in them to perform what was requested, and it was in the spirit of knowing he would do what he said he would. That Is why Mary said in verse 38 says Behold, the maidservant of the Lord! Let it be to me according to you WORD." It was in his WORD that he would establish it!

Mathew 5:37 "But let your YES be YES and your NO be NO."

2 Corinthians 1:20 "For all the promises of God in Him are Yes, and in Him Amen, To the Glory of God through us."

1 Corinthians 2:9-12 "Eye as not seen nor ear heard nor have entered into the heart of man, the things which God has prepared for those who love him."

Ephesians 1:17-18 "That the God of our Lord Jesus Christ, the father of Glory, may give you the spirit of wisdom and revelation in the knowledge of Him. Therefore, I pray the eyes (THE YES OF YOUR UNDERSTANDING) of your understanding being enlightened that you ma knows the hope of you calling, what are the riches of the glory of His inheritance in the saints."

Psalms 20:4 "May he grants you according to your heart's desire and fulfill all your purpose. You will rejoice in your salvation! And in the name of your God, you will set up your banners! May the Lord fulfill all your petitions?' (Requests)

Phil 1:6 "Being confident of this very thing that He who has begun a good work in you will complete it until the day of Jesus Christ!"

2 Timothy 1:9 "Who has saves us and called us with a holy calling, not according to our works, but according to His own purpose and grace which was given to us in Christ Jesus before time began."

Preparation for his kingdom, just as the King called forth women to be prepared to try to win His heart, just as Esther consecrated and set herself apart to win the heart of the King and favor. King Jesus desired you since the foundations to prepare your heart to receive Him. The greatest gift you can give Him is your heart and your YES TO YOUR KINGDOM PURPOSE. That is what you have been prepared for!

Time to **REFLECT:** Look over your life; how are some ways or things you see where God may be calling you to come closer to him? What are your desires in this journey that you long to see fulfilled? What are some areas you need to let go of and trust God?

_____

_____

_____

_____

_____

_____

_____

_____

Jeremiah 29:11 "For I know the plans I have for you, declares the Lord, plans to prosper you and not to harm you, plans to give you hope and a future."

Chapter 8

Worthy is the Call

I want to minister to you about being worthy of the call. In order to fulfill purpose and destiny, we must be confident in who we are in Christ; gaining confidence grows as our walk in the Lord grows. As we see his faithfulness and love for us, we begin to have confidence in our creator and knowing that he is for us in every season of our life, and through all our ups and downs, knowing he is our comforter and counselor. We must come to and understand that he is the one that created and called us for this time.

John 14-16 "And I will ask the Father, and he will give you another advocate to help you and be with you forever."

Isaiah 30:15 "In stillness and quietness shall be your strength."

If you do not already know, he wants you to gain confidence about yourself in him!

As women of God, no matter what season we walk through, whether we are on the mountain top or in the valley low, we are enduring and encountering purpose.

Romans 8:28 "And we know that all things, work together for the good of those who love God, to those who are called according to

His purpose."

While we are in those valley seasons, we are building our faith muscles and producing character and patience, and long-suffering. Things tend to happen to us that throw us off course and make us feel unworthy of the call, but no matter what has happened in your life, God still wants to use you; you are significant to him for the work and plan; of the kingdom! He wants to encourage you, no matter where you are at in this season of your life or because of past seasons, that you will continue to allow him to lead you by his grace and his unconditional love to fulfill Purpose in your life and take your mess and make it your message.

Revelation 12:11 "And they overcame him by the blood of the Lamb and by the word of their testimony, and they did not love their lives to the death."

What is your message, what we have endured in the process, what he did for us, how we got to where we are now? Even if at times when you felt like you had failed over and over. Let Him continue to grace you for each mistake, each failure, each change. Let him continue the work in you to transform you more and more into his image from glory to glory!

Romans 4:23 "For all have sinned and fall short of the glory of God."

Isaiah 64:6 "All of us have become like one who Is unclean, and all our righteous acts are like filthy rags; we all shrivel up like a leaf, and like the wind, our sins sweep us away."

You women of God are deemed WORTHY!

Worthy is having worth, merit, or value, to be considered useful—honorable and deserving, Important, virtuous, of high station high position.

They are chosen for admission, righteous, which is in right standing with God.

God has already deemed you WORTHY since the foundations of the earth!

Worthy is the Call!

A call is to announce authoritatively, proclaim order into effect, establish or summon by divine demand. To summon an office or mandate.

To cause to come, to designate or demand someone to fulfill a promise. Covenant in which we agree and with alignment with God's ultimate plan for creation. Who we are, ordered to fulfill something while we are here?

An experience of divine appointment to a vocation. To be called a minister or ambassador of the gospel, a request or invitation.

To summon, to require for service or action.

God loves to beckon and woo us into deeper commitment and relationship in him and the call to be an ambassador for him and a disciple of Christ.

Calling is a strong inner impulse toward a particular course of action, especially when accompanied by conviction of divine influence. A vocation to which one is called, and activities performed. We desire to become all we can be because we are in love with him.

Eph 4:1 To walk worthy of the calling "I, therefore, a prisoner of the Lord, beseech you to walk worthy of your calling with which you were called."

Rom 11:29 "The Gifts and calling are irrevocable."

There are great gifts and talents He has placed within you that have yet to be discovered.

1 Corinthians 1:26-28 "For you see your calling, brethren that not many wise according to the flesh, not many mighty, not many nobles are called. But God has chosen the foolish things for the world to put to shame the things of the world to put to shame the mighty things.

And the base thing of the world and the things which are despised God has chosen, and the things which are not to bring to nothing the things that are."

God loves to use ordinary women to do great things, to make a difference, and influence.

1 Corinthian 7:20 "Remain in the calling in which you were called."

Ephesians 4:4-7, 11-12 "There is one body and one spirit just as you were called on one hope of your calling. One Lord, one faith, one baptism. One God and Father of all, who is above all, was given according to the measure of Christ's gift. And He himself gave some prophets some evangelists and some pastors and teachers, for the equipping of the saints for the work of the ministry and the edifying of the body of Christ."

Some of you are called to the fivefold ministry, and the rest are just as important to help make a difference wherever you are. God needs and desires you!

2 Timothy 1:9 "Who has saved us and calls us with a holy calling not according to our works, but according to his own purpose and grace which was given to us in Christ Jesus before time began."

God desires that you fulfill all his purposes in you.

Psalms 20:4 "May He grants you according to your heart's desire and fulfills all your purpose."

A promise is something favorable to come, expectation, a vow, giving assurance, commitment.

Mathew 6:33 "But seek first the kingdom of God and His righteousness, and all these things shall be added to you."

We feel unworthy because we take on our past and the things the world and society put on us, yet we were made in the image of Christ and deemed worthy as he is worthy and to take our rightful place in the kingdom!

To understand Purpose, we need to know how to walk out the process, and we must realize we are in the time frame of God for our lives. For the sake of the Kingdom. We are not just mortal bodies but spiritual beings with the capacity to function with authority in the realm of the spirit. To reign here and take dominion while we are here to fulfill our God-given assignments.

Purpose is to make a difference wherever we are positioned for that time and season of our life, making a difference and influencing the kingdom. We are ambassadors of Christ. We rule and reign for him.

Purpose is always a process, some seasons are good, and some are more difficult, but when you have a purpose, you have a passion; therefore, when things get tough, you know you still have somewhere to go and something to fulfill. It is called **PURPOSE**.

Habakkuk 2:2 "Write the vision and make it plain on tablets that he may run who reads it, for the vision is yet for an appointed time. But in the end, it will speak, and it will not lie. Therefore, though it tarries, wait for it because it will surely come it will not tarry."

Do not despise what you must work with, start right where you are at with what you have and watch him MULTIPLY IT!

Zechariah 4:10 "Do not despise these small beginnings, for the Lord rejoices to see the work begin, to see the plumb line in Zerubbabel's hand."

He desires to see the work in you begin!

God does not call the equipped; he equips the call. Equipping is a process, making fit, preparing, training, making fully qualified for service, and making the necessary adjustments needed to function properly!

We need to understand there are mandates, callings, and giftings upon our lives to help equip us for ministry work. Ministry does not necessarily mean the five-fold ministry functions of full-time ministers, apostles, prophets' teachers, pastors, and evangelists. You are all ministers because you are ambassadors and Disciples of Christ: therefore, your area of influence is your ministry!

Some of you may feel called to full-time ministry or functions. Yet, destiny is still learning to walk through and endure the process, even as we have talked in the past about Esther and what it took for her to fulfill her PURPOSE.

God has the same anointing on many of you, and An Esther and a Deborah anointing, and he is waiting for you to believe in yourself and to rise up in these last days to come out of hiding with your gifts and your callings and to take your rightful stand in your places of authority and area of influences!

I pray that every gift is stirred up, the gifts of prophecy, exhortation, the gift of preaching, teaching, and evangelizing; I pray right now that the holy spirit would begin to arrest you and affirm who you are in this season.

I pray every gift doormat or unknown to you that is locked up to be opened for the purposes of God. I pray for the gift of healing to begin to flow, I pray for prophetic sounds and song, and dance and utterance began to flow in and through you, that you would get excited about who you are, knowing you are worthy of the call right now in Jesus Mighty Name.

Time to **REFLECT:** Do you desire God's purposes to be developed in your journey while here on earth? Even when it gets hard, will you reflect on how God will turn it around for your good and His GLORY!

_____

_____

_____

_____

_____

_____

_____

Romans 8:28 "And we know that in all things God works for the good of those who love him, who have been called according to His purpose."

Chapter 9

Victorious Women

There are three women in the bible that I would like to focus on in this chapter: anointed, appointed, and victorious women in the Bible, Deborah, Mary, and Esther.

Victory: A success or triumph over an enemy in battle or war. An engagement is ending in triumph. The ultimate and decisive superiority in any battle. Success over an opponent and opposition or difficulty.

These women all had something in common; they all submitted their will to God and came out on top!

Purpose kept pulling them forth, therefore in every season, they were victorious because they were always in the right place at the right time, they submitted their wills unto God, even in their difficult times or what deemed to be impossible. They continued to trust and say YES. And favor pulled them to the other side of the next phase or season of victory and purpose.

Matthew 19:26 "With men this is impossible, but with God all things are possible."

Destiny: Something that is to happen or has happened to a

particular person or thing. A predetermined, inevitable, or irresistible course of events or circumstances.

See, it is all about a heart attitude, even when things are not going your way. Will you submit it?

Even when you know not what to do, will you continue to stand, believe and trust the father's plan.

Submission: Act of submitting to the power of another. State of being submissive or compliant, meekness. Submitting something of consideration.

The same Holy Spirit who enabled these delivers to do great exploits and fulfill the Lord's plans and purposes is still currently at work. He desires to move upon His people so that they can do impossible things. The Lord wants to bring deliverance to His people; He is looking for consecrated women whom he can empower with His spirit. The Lord wants you to learn how to be victorious in battle by depending on Him.

God wants to raise up women who will be deliverers, judges, and servants to change their area of influence. We must learn to be victorious in our own lives to help deliver and help others be victorious in their lives.

Deborah was considered a Judge: *Judge is to govern, pass judgment, and pronounce.*

Deborah helped make a difference to those around her; she was strong and victorious; therefore, she was able to help others to be victorious.

The key to Deborah's effectiveness was her spiritual commitment and walked with God.

She was able to fulfill God's plans and purposes for her life even through times of warfare because of her submission to the call.

Women are victorious when they get an understanding that God is really for them and not against them. God created them with a plan in mind and a purpose to fulfill.

You will be victorious when you understand why you are here, but you must realize you were created with purpose before the difficult times come. You must know your vision and God-given desire so that when the difficult times come you know without a doubt you have somewhere to go and something to fulfill!

You keep your focus on what's ahead, not looking back but looking forward! Pressing toward the high calling of God, the mark.

Philippians 3:13 "Brethren I do not count myself to have apprehended, but one thing I do forgetting those things which are behind and reaching forward to those things which are ahead. I press toward the goal for the prize of the upward call of God in Christ Jesus." (Which is the purpose)

You learn to keep your momentum and keep your endurance, and you are pressing, pushing through the obstacles, and exercising those faith muscles to take you to another level; you have your hand always stretched out and ready to grab the goal!

They persevere till they see their breakthrough! Victorious women also know when it is time to rest in the Lord and know he has already won the battle.

Esther was another strong woman filled with purpose and destiny; Esther, through all her loss and pain, was chosen for such a time; she only had to get through the process of her pain and loss so she could move forward into an appointed time where purpose and destiny would meet. Because of her sacrifice and obedience, she was able to deliver a whole nation. (People prepared for you to reach and minister to)

Often, we cannot see the potential that lies within us. Sometimes, we see our present circumstances, pain, and hurt. Yet God has something far better and greater on the other side for us. We only need to keep moving and keep going; we need endurance, perseverance, and a tenacity that will push us to stretch the extra mile until we see our breakthrough!

Victorious women are not women that win every battle in their life, there victorious because they have an understanding that there will be some pain, and some loss along the way, yet they know how to get back up and keep going, they know there is something deep down on the inside of them that Is causing them to press through the storms of life. They know that as they are pressing, they are becoming stronger, and there is purpose still being developed in their situations and circumstances. They know how to lean unto God and allow Him to direct their ways.

Proverbs 3:5 "Lean not unto your own understanding, but in all of your ways acknowledge God, and he will direct your steps."

Another victorious woman was Mary; she was young at age, yet still chosen and handpicked by God himself. She did not struggle with what was asked of her but said… *Luke 1:38 "Behold the maidservant of the Lord! Let it be to me according to your word, and the angel departed from her."*

Your age does not matter; even if you are a young adult, God desires to raise you up and give you purpose at a young age so he can use you for His Glory!

Because of her willingness and trust, she carried one of the greatest miracles ever told. God has great things in store for each of us, and he sees the unlocked potential that we have yet to discover or see. It does not mean we will win every battle; it just means that God has a great purpose and believes in us. And if God is for us, who could surely be against us! So, allow God to develop and strengthen you; let him be your greatest encourager when everyone else doubts you or what you are capable of accomplishing. God knows how to write upon our hearts, and he is the author and finisher of our faith.

Hebrews 12:2 "Looking unto Jesus, the author, and finisher of our faith, who for the joy that was set before Him endured the cross, despising the shame, and has sat down at the right hand of the throne of God."

I believe God has something great just for you to do! I think that you are significant to his plan and purpose, and you are one of a kind, unique, gifted, and celebrated! He is just waiting for you to take that next step into purpose!

He is waiting for you to believe in yourself and look to him where your help comes from. He is for you and not against you.

Psalms 122:1 "I will lift up my eyes to the hills, from whence comes my help? My help comes from the Lord, who made heaven and earth."

Time to **REFLECT:** What areas have you conquered and seen growth? What can you do to allow God to help you be more Victorious in other areas of your life, relationships, children, marriage, job, etc.?

_____

_____

_____

_____

_____

_____

_____

Mathew 19:26 Jesus looked at them and said, "With man this is impossible, but with God all things are possible."

Chapter 10

From Tragedy to Triumph

As we begin to close in these last chapters, I pray that you understand why it is so important to pursue your purpose passionately.

Let me explain something, and you will never be satisfied to the fullest in life without Christ at the very center and core of who you are. No relationship includes marriage, friendships, jobs, hobbies, or pursuits; none of it will fulfill you. Do not get me wrong, it may for a season, or you may even be content at times, but without Him, there will always be a void, something missing, you will always question or feel there must be more to life than just this.

Isaiah 43:7 "Bring all who claim me as their God, for I have made them for my Glory. It was I who created them."

He will always have your best interest at heart, no matter what you have gone through or the places you have come from or the choices you have made; he desires to redeem you from the hardships we encounter on this journey we call life. It does not mean it will always be easy on the contrary, but it will be WORTH IT!

Isaiah 55:8-9 "For my thoughts are not your thoughts, nor are your ways My ways," says the Lord. *"For as the heavens are higher than the earth, so are My ways higher than your ways, And My thoughts than your thoughts."*

He will even take the very things you think you crave and desire that you think you need but are really causing you more pain like drugs, alcohol, toxic relationships, etc. Whatever it is that comes between you and Him, and His desire is for you to come into your full potential and thrive, not just survive!

The purpose is not always on some grand scale, and it is simply giving what you have back to the Lord, giving his investment which is YOU, back with a return. Including your giftings and talents that he has placed within you. You are dedicating what is yours to Him.

Romans 11:29-31 "God does not take back his gifts. He does not change his mind about those he has chosen. At one time, you did not obey God. But now you have received mercy because Israel did not obey. In the same way, Israel has not been obeying God. But now they receive mercy Because of God's mercy to you."

James 1:17-18 "Every good and perfect gift is from above, coming down from the Father of the heavenly lights, whom there is no change or shifting shadow. He chose to give us birth through the word of truth, that we would be a kind of firstfruits of His creation."

YOU are created for PURPOSE! ON PURPOSE! He PASSIONATELY PERSUES YOU!

Whatever you have been through, and let me reassure you, we all have had stuff in our lives we do not like others to see or know about, or that make us feel ashamed, disgraced, or disgusted at parts of our lives and that are messy. But it is time to take the masks of rejection, betrayal, abandonment, and hatred off so we can embrace what we have been through and allow it to shape us into who we are becoming.

TRAGEDY is an event causing great suffering, destruction, and distress, such as a serious accident, A tragic event, an unhappy ending, a bad event that causes great sadness, even death. A sorrowful situation!

Does this sound like anything you have encountered in your life so far? I have, I have had many things that have shaken my world to the core! But I finally surrendered and allowed God to turn those situations in my life around for growth and to use it toward my Purpose to help others. I embrace my story now!

He can turn around your darkest season of loss, heartache, and even your self-sabotage.

Yes, I said it; sometimes, we sabotage our self because of FEAR. We do not feel worthy to receive goodness, so we self-sabotage. I used to be good at that in my life, but not anymore; I learned that FEAR is a false reality appearing to seem real most of the time. Sometimes we run from our calling and purpose feeling inadequate, so we rebel or run out of fear! We then learn to trust as our faith grows during and after each struggle as we see how faithful He is even when we have not been faithful. *Hebrews 5:8 "Son though he was, he learned obedience from what he suffered."* God did not intend for us to go through all that we went through; he grieves, hurts just as we do, and does not like to see any of his children hurting but will turn it around!

2 Timothy 1:7 "For the Spirit God gave us does not make us timid, but gives us power, love, and self-discipline."

FEAR-A feeling of anxiety concerning the outcome of something.

Isaiah 41:10 "So do not fear, for I am with you; do not be dismayed, for I am your God. I will strengthen you and help you.; I will uphold you with my righteous right hand."

Let your tragedy become your triumph! Let it be a turning point from that mess to your message, that can now be a tool to encourage and inspire other women that they too are not alone. We have all been through something that has caused some tragedy in our life by now, and if you have been lucky this far not to have had to endure the crisis, at some point you will, it is just part of life and humanity because we live in a fallen world. God wants to take what you have been through and to use it for his glory! God can work that tragedy you have been through and turn it into something beautiful if you let him. You will go from tragedy to triumph, from a victim mentality to victorious in him. When I look back now over the tragedies in my life, all the heartache and loss, I realize I grew the most during these times though I could not see it while I was in it.

Ecclesiastes 3:11 "He has made everything beautiful in its time. He has also set eternity in the human heart, yet no one can fathom what God has done from beginning to end."

I have learned so much more wisdom and my greatest strengths;

now that I have endured and come out of those things, I am so grateful, not for the pain or loss; no one cares to take a loss! No one willingly wants to go through a hard divorce, addiction, loss of relationships, loss of a loved one, bankruptcy, etc. But when we learn to embrace where we are and who we are in these moments and surrender to God, he can and will sustain us and get us through these difficult times. Allow the breaking, and it's ok to be real with who you are in these tough moments of your life. You can trust him with your heart, thoughts, and pain, He wants to restore and heal those deep wounds and areas of your life that you are ashamed of or run from, yet all of it is a part of who you are and who you are becoming. None of us like the withered or ugly parts of our lives; I have learned in seasons past not to resist where I have been or what I have lost but to embrace the growth and the new. Purpose never stopped chasing me because life happened; it did not catch God by surprise. And though I may have set purpose aside in some seasons or left it behind, I eventually knew that purpose was still calling me, so I picked it back up. And I believe if you are reading this book, it is because Purpose is calling YOU!

Jeremiah 29:11 "For I know the plans I have for you, declares the Lord, plans for welfare and not for evil, to give you a future and a hope."

It does not mean we will not still have difficult times; it just means we can get through anything with Him by our side and still find purpose.

Romans 8:31 "What, then, shall l we say in response to these things?

If God is for us, who can be against us?"

When we have encountered some loss, shame, or tragedy, the enemy tries to produce fear, fear of the future. He tries to make us question if we have a purpose. Therefore, we must face our fears of the past and present and push toward the mark of the high calling in Christ!

Philippians 3:14 "I press on toward the goal to win the prize for which God has called me heavenward in Christ."

2 Corinthians 4:8-9 "We are hard-pressed on every side, but not crushed; perplexed, but not in despair. Persecuted, but not abandoned; struck down, but not destroyed."

He is developing you for goodness and greatness so that you can make a difference in your area of influence!

It does not mean we are perfect, but we are being perfected in Him as we yield and surrender the shattered pieces of our lost hopes and dreams and let Him renew and restore our vision so that he can birth something new in you; with what you have left!

Finding and developing purpose gives us the lord's joy, which becomes our greatest strength and helps us conquer everyday living!

It is a continual bubbling over of the goodness of God.

Psalm 28:7 "The Lord is my strength and my shield' my heart trusts In Him, and I am helped. My heart leaps for joy, and I will give thanks to him in song. The Lord is the strength of his people, a fortress of salvation for his anointed one. Save your people and bless Your inheritance; be their shepherd and carry them forever."

Had it not been for his mercy and grace, most of us would not be still standing! And if you are still here, then you still have PURPOSE!

John 10:10 "The thief comes only to steal and kill and destroy; I have come that they may have life and have it to the full."

The enemy wants you to give up! He wants you to abort your assignment and your call! He comes to still the very seed of purpose in you, and He knows if you ever discover who you really are, you will cause him a lot of damage to his Kingdom of darkness!

So let God have your rejection, shame, guilt, loss, and brokenness, and let him take you from TRAGEDY TO TRIUMPH! No matter where you have been or what you have done, or what has happened to you, God has not changed his mind about you! He is not disgusted or ashamed of your past or possibly even your present or even your future. He has still chosen you; He still desires you, and he still equips you for His Kingdom purposes!

Psalm 27:13 "I remain confident of this; I will see the goodness of the LORD in the land of the living."

I once had a strong mentor in my life that when I did not think what I had was important, or enough she would encourage me and say, "There is more than enough room for you to bring your portion to the king's table and dine with him." So let me encourage you to bring what you have, bring your AUTHENTIC self; you are more than enough! We need your portion!

You must go from tragedy to triumph and forgive others, and you must forgive yourself, which can sometimes be the hardest thing.

We, at times, like to blame ourselves for events that have happened in our lives that may or may not be our doing, forgive forgive forgive! Forgiveness releases you to move forward!

Mathew 6:14 "For if you forgive other people when they sin against you, your heavenly Father will also forgive you."

Forgive and go forward into your FUTURE!

1 Corinthians 15:55-57 "Where, O death, is your victory? Where, O death, is your sting?

The sting of death is sin, and the power of sin is the law. But thanks be to God! He gives us the victory through our Lord Jesus Christ."

TRIUMPH-To have a great victory or achievement. To win! A feeling of satisfaction.

Psalm 34:8 "Taste and see that the Lord is good, blessed is the one who takes refuge in Him."

Even when the closest people to you chose to leave you, reject you, abuse or abandon you, GOD IS STILL WITH YOU!

He is more than enough even to start over…...

TIME TO *REFLECT: What are some tragedies that you have gone through that you still need to give to God so you can heal? What or who do you need to forgive, include yourself? Are you willing to allow God to use your mess for his message and for His Glory? Spend some time reflecting on where you were to where you are and what you would like to see change. Ask God to help you with this and be authentic. He already knows… write a prayer from your heart to God show me your PURPOSE.*

_____

_____

_____

_____

_____

_____

_____

Romans 8:28 "And we know that in all things God works for the good of those who love him, who have been called according to his purpose."

The whole earth is waiting for you to manifest into your God-given purpose!

Chapter 11

When Purpose Pursues YOU

What do you do when Purpose begins to pursue you? You yield to it! You embrace it! You move with it! How do you know when Purpose is now seeking you? You begin to experience uncommon FAVOR with GOD and man. Blessings begin to chase you down. Miracles, signs, and wonders follow you!

You begin to encounter DIVINE connections; you align with God-ordained assignments and relationships. You are provoked to do more than you usually would to bear good fruit for the days and seasons to come. You embrace the pruning necessary, so you can step into your next season even when the process is uncomfortable. Your YES to GOD has become much louder! You are willing to bear your cross for the sake of Christ. You are not worried about pleasing man but pleasing God! You become the more AUTHENTIC YOU THAT WAS CREATED FOR A GREATER PURPOSE. With all your strengths and weakness, you decide to use it for his Purpose and Glory.

Matthew 16:24-26 "Then Jesus told his disciples, "If anyone would come after me, let him deny himself and take up his cross and follow me. For whoever would save his life will lose it, but whoever loses his life for my sake will find it. For what will it profit a man if he gains the whole world and forfeits his soul? Or what shall a man give in return for his soul?"

Some things must die so they can live; you are probably asking, what do you mean some things have to die so that they can live? I will give an example of what I mean since Christ spoke in parables to get his point across.

I used to take long country drives every evening to talk with the Lord and silence my mind. When I went through a crisis that shook my world, I felt shattered at that moment. My country drives came to a halt. I had lost it all. While writing this book after seven years, the Lord prompted me to take another country drive; by this time, as I listened, he told me "Just because you thought your dreams and desires had died in the past season, and you thought that *purpose* had died with it" "New life will begin to spring forth and what appeared to die, purpose is still living on the inside of you."

John 12:24 "Most assuredly, I say to you, unless a grain of wheat falls into the ground and dies, it remains alone; but if it dies, it produces much grain."

Psalm 23:6 "Surely goodness and mercy shall fallow me All the days of my life; And I will dwell in the house of the Lord Forever."

This is where PURPOSE and DESTINY begin to COLLIDE!

1 Corinthians 2:9-But as it is written: "Eye has not seen, nor ear heard, Nor have entered into the heart of man The things which God has prepared for those who love Him."

You begin to realize you are in a prominent season and stepping into a prominent place! With more potential to meet other prominent people in prominent places and helping you to full fill your purpose. They become tools and gifts to help assist in what God is calling you to do for Him! You begin to exchange with other like-minded people who either have the same purpose or agenda as you or people who have what you need in this season to help you fulfill your assignment or ministry. They may have resources that you can use. Sometimes it could be financially to help promote your vision, and it can also simply be resources of wisdom or access to things you did not have before. God uses people to help you connect and fulfill your desire's.

Psalm 37:4 "Delight yourself also in the Lord, And He shall give you the desires of your heart."

A lot of times when you have a deep desire it is God's desire, he is placing within you!

I live with purpose on purpose now because of the loss and what remains. I have learned to appreciate what I have left. I enjoy life and others. It is far from perfect, and I have moments and seasons just as we all do. But, I see how each part of our journey can birth something new if we allow it!

John 12:24 "Most assuredly, I say to you, unless a grain of wheat falls into the ground and dies, it remains alone, but if it dies, it produces much grain."

Isaiah 55:8-9 "For My thoughts are not your thoughts, nor are your ways My ways," says the Lord. "For as the heavens are higher than the earth, so are My ways higher than your ways, and My thoughts than your thoughts."

If God asks something of you, he will give you the provision for the vision! He will provide you with creative and witty ideas to produce what you require, even when it feels like you have nothing left to offer.

That is why we need to lean into the Lord for direction and directives for each season we encounter, but especially a prominent season, we want to be able to access all that God has for us in a season like this! When a window of opportunity opens, we need to yield to it if we know God is doing it!

It is such an extraordinary moment in time when we have seasons like these in our lives. After all the drought or dark times in our lives, we should take the time to enjoy the season God has brought us to in times like these!

Ecclesiastes 3:1-8 "To everything there is a season, A time for every purpose under heaven: A time to be born, and a time to die; A time to plant, and a time to pluck what is planted; A time to kill,

and a time to heal; A time to break down, and a time to build up; A time to weep, and a time to laugh;

A time to mourn, and a time to dance; A time to cast away stones, and a time to gather stones; A time to embrace, and a time to refrain from embracing; A time to gain, and a time to lose; A time to keep,

and a time to throw away; A time to tear, and a time to sew; A time to keep silence, and a time to speak; A time to love, and a time to hate; A time of war, and a time of peace."

Even now as I began to align myself in a prominent season and yield. The sound of purpose becomes LOUDER, and the lies of the enemy become quieter....

Psalm 61:1-5, 8 "Hear my cry, O God; Attend to my prayer. From the end of the earth, I will cry to You, when my heart is overwhelmed; Lead me to the rock that is higher than I. For You have been a shelter for me, A strong tower from the enemy. I will abide in Your tabernacle forever; I will trust in the shelter of Your wings. Selah For You, O God, have heard my vows; You have given me the heritage of those who fear Your name... So, I will sing praise to Your name forever, That I may daily perform my vows."

Psalm 46:10 "Be still, and know that I am God"

I want to encourage you that all the pain and adversity will work itself out when God is for you, who can be against you!

Romans 8:31 "What shall we then say to these things? If God be for us, who can be against us?"

In my journey through it all, I know this is what I was created for, to encourage and minister to others, to be a reconciler to the heart of the father.

We do not just wake up one day and we're in purpose; we are being propelled into purpose over the years through all we encounter in life. That is why it is so important to embrace who you are, to love yourself in your strengths and weaknesses. The sooner you come to terms with who you are, and you are worthy and lovable and created on purpose for his purpose, the sooner you can begin to yield to what he has for you!

We grow and gain experience by what we have been through and what we have overcome!

Let me encourage you, YOU ARE AN OVERCOMER!

Romans 12:21 "Do not be overcome by evil but overcome evil with good."

When you desire to know who you are and why you are here and begin to passionately pursue purpose long enough, PURPOSE will eventually pursue YOU!

That is what is happening in my season right now! I have passionately pursued purpose for so long that now it is pursuing ME!

Proverbs 8:35 "For whoever finds me finds life and obtains favor from the Lord."

Trust me when I say I can relate to some of your pain, heartache, rejection, betrayal, and probably so much more! It may not be easy, but it will be WORTH IT!

You will begin to understand more about your pain and how it helped shaped you. As purpose pursues you, and you allow your story to become an opportunity to help others wherever your story may lead; yield and say YES!

You have been through too much to waste it; you have too much wisdom, insight, and knowledge to share with others.

Proverbs 3:1-2 "Trust in the Lord with all your heart and lean not on your own understanding; In all your ways acknowledge Him, And He shall direct your paths."

TIME TO REFLECT-What is your TESTimony? What is it that you have overcome? Have you been pursuing purpose and if not why? Do you desire to know your PURPOSE for the Kingdom? Do you think purpose is pursuing YOU, why or why not? What is your Message? Ask the Lord to take what you have left and multiply it!

_____

_____

_____

_____

_____

_____

_____

Genesis 1:28 "Then God blessed them, and God said to them, be fruitful and multiply, fill the earth and subdue it, have dominion over the fish of the sea, over the birds of the air, and over every living thing that moves on the earth."

Chapter 12

I am a Gift

When we open who we are to the Lord, we begin to discover gifts in us we never knew we had for his purposes. So, I want you to mutter and ponder over this last chapter. At the end of this book, I desire that passion will be stirred within you. Maybe you lost your fire that flamed in a past season! Mabey life quenched the desires of your heart and stole your vision of how you once thought it should be or look like?

God still has a purpose for you even when you may feel everything is dormant or dead in some areas of your life! So, Mabey, you were once aware of what God had placed in you, but you set purpose down for a season and never quite picked it back up?

As we close out the last chapter of this book, my prayer for you is that this book would be a catalyst that will birth a new chapter in your life!

Luke 1:37 "For with God nothing will be impossible."

Where you thought you could not be used, is exactly the opposite of His desire to use you!

Psalm 59:16 "But I will sing of Your power; Yes, I will sing aloud of

Your mercy in the morning;

For You have been my defense and refuge in the day of my trouble."

He wants you to open what he has given you, **GIFTS**.

Luke 11:13 "If you then, being evil, know how to give good gifts to your children, how much more will your heavenly Father give the Holy Spirit to those who ask Him!"

When you begin to open the gifts, he has given you, and he can then use you as a GIFT to others!

Mabey, you are not sure what your gifts or talents are. But, as you ask and receive, you will begin to see the manifestation of what's inside of you!

Mabey, you are called as an Intercessor, to pray on behalf of others for Kingdom Purposes and assignments!

Mabey your called into the area of helps to help others with their vision, to help with your time, assistance, or financially.

Or a Prophet to tear down and build back up, to declare and decree, and to establish the heart of God!

To hear the heart of God for people and places! To war against darkness that tries to cover the earth and people's lives!

Or maybe you have a desire or gift or talent to play an instrument or sing or dance....to write?

These are just a few I have mentioned here, yet there are many gifts and talents out there that God has placed in us, uniquely given for your personality and how he created you; you must want to discover and open your gift!

As you discover the gifts and talents in you and you use them, you will begin to see other skills and talents that you did not see before!

God will give you the grace to operate in the area that you have been called to.

When you discover the gift in you, it comes with pruning and equips to make you more skilled in that area of influence you are called upon.

1 Corinthians 1:27 "But God has chosen the foolish things of the world to put to shame the wise, and God has chosen the weak things of the world to put to shame the things which are mighty."

Embrace yourself! Embrace who you are! Embrace your GIFT! And declare after me.

I AM A GIFT!

After all the Lord has blessed us with, the last thing we want to do is bury or hide our gifts and talents, we want him to multiply what we have!

Matthew 25:14-30 tells us ... The parable of the Talents talks about how a master trusted his servants with talents. Some servants used their talents and increased with more talents. The other servant held on to his talent, hiding it and returned with still only one talent. The parable is used to express how we should use what God has given us, that He may develop and increase what we have.

Matthew 5:15-16 "Nor do they light a lamp and put it under a basket, but on a lampstand, and it gives light to all who are in the house. Let your light so shine before men, that they may see your good works and glorify your Father in heaven."

TIME TO *REFLECT: Do you know what your gifts and talents are? Do you desire to know? Do you desire to be used by God? Quietly say a prayer from your heart to God and ask him to open opportunities for you to share what you have that you may be a GIFT to others! Trust me it will be a GREAT REWARD to give and see others blessed with what you have!*

_____

_____

_____

_____

_____

_____

_____

_____

Matthew 25:21 "His lord said to him, 'Well done, good and faithful servant; you were faithful over a few things, I will make you ruler over many things. Enter into the joy of your lord."

You can contact the author for speaking engagements, conferences and ministry products.

Valerie Tasi

(580) 917-3502

Email Address:

Tasi00@yahoo.com

Made in the USA
Columbia, SC
14 October 2021

46926971R00057